This **book** belongs to
a girl who is unique and **talented**
and **brave** and real and
who has everything it takes
to make her **dreams**
come true:

_____

(your name here)

Titles by Ashley Rice
Published by
Blue Mountain Arts®

For an Incredible Kid
Girl Power
Girls Rule
Make Your Dreams Come True
Sisters Are Forever Friends
Use Your Girl Power
You Are a Girl Who Can Do Anything
You Are a Girl Who Totally Rocks!
You Go, Girl... Keep Dreaming

For an Incredible Girl/Para una niña increíble
(Bilingual Edition)

Library of Congress Control Number: 2014951611
ISBN: 978-1-59842-865-0

▼ and Blue Mountain Press are registered in U.S. Patent and Trademark Office.
Certain trademarks used under license.

Printed in China.
First Printing: 2015

Blue Mountain Arts, Inc.
P.O. Box 4549, Boulder, Colorado 80306

Make YOUR DReams come TRUe

A Girl's Guide to Always Believing in Yourself

Ashley Rice

Blue Mountain Press ™

Boulder, Colorado

An Introduction
by Penelope J. Miller

Hi! My name is Penelope J. Miller, and I am the narrator of this book. I'm excited that I get to tell you what it is about and to make the journey through its pages right alongside you.

The drawings and writings in this book were created to encourage girls like you to follow their dreams and be who they are. It's important to be yourself, believe in yourself, and be the star of your own life. It's also important for you to know that there will be lots of times when you mess up. Sometimes I think we don't try new things because we are afraid that we won't be immediately successful or perfect.

It seems to me the only way you can get where you are going is by jumping over each and every hurdle along the way, even if on the first round you miss each and every one.

When the path to my dreams is a little bumpy, I figure things out by writing my thoughts down. Maybe your way of figuring out things — and your dreams — has to do with math or gymnastics or science. Maybe you figure things out about your life by talking to people or by playing soccer. It doesn't matter; the world is full of ideas and each person brings something special to the world that no one else can bring. This is what I say to that whole idea: hang on to your dreams and give your life everything you've got.

So anyway, I hope that wherever you are, you're doing well — and that you always believe in your dreams.

your friend,

Penelope J.

You Can Make
Your Dreams Come True

In this **world**...
wishing you:
a little peace
 a little **love**
a little  luck
a little sunshine
a little **happiness**
a little fun...

...and as far
as reaching your
dreams
and goals?

You can do it!

You can make your
dreams
come true!

Penelope's Keys to Unlocking Your Potential

Dance and laugh hard
and grin a lot
in your **heart.**
Follow your dREamS
(it's always worth it).
Don't ever stop **smiling.**
Don't **ever** stop trying.
Stay on your toes.
Reach out as far as
you can reach
and then reach **farther.**
Don't forget to
ROCK the world.
And — oh yeah:
shine on.

Your Spirit Will Lead the Way

Your **spirit** is like your heart —
when you reach up or out,
it helps you **fly**.
Your spirit can be your **love**
for different people or things —
it'll **lift** you way up
if you fall sometimes.
Your spirit says:
"**Don't ever** give up,"
"I'm in your corner,"
and "**Let's go!**"

YOUR **spirit cheers**
for your hopes
and dreams.
It can pull you
through anything.
It will **keep** you strong.

You Are a Rainbow in the Sky

You are an extra-special somebody.

You are a beautiful butterfly.

You are the favorite flavor of the bunch...

like double-chocolate-cherry pie.

You are
an angel,

a joker,

and a **mystery**
that never lies.

Like a **dream**
sent to the
stars,
you are...

a **rainbow** in the sky.

Some Words About You:

amazing

wonderful

electrifying

cute

killer-smart

dazzling

one-of-a-kind

You are
one of the great
girls I know!

Believe in Yourself

Believe in the way that you are
and the way you will be.
Believe in the things that you say.
The WORLD is yours to see.

16

And if you should go,
if you should turn around one day,
if you should ever doubt your dreams
in any way,
don't think twice about it.
Don't worry too long
about whether you'll find a place
for yourself in the world — you belong.
You'll get where
you're going someday.
For no matter what happens,
you will find a way.
Believe in the way that you are
and the way you will be.
You are a shining star
in this world.

Penelope's One and Only Rule You Need to Follow

As you go through this **woRld**,
if you want to make youR way
as a **staR**...

do the **best** you can.

Get Rid of Self-Doubt

Self-doubt is a lot like brain freeze...

your brain, cold →

think about something else...

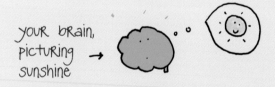

your brain, picturing sunshine →

...and it will eventually go away.

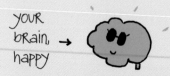

your brain, happy →

You have the POWER within yourself
to make good decisions. You have
the beauty within yourself to live a
wonderful life. You have the courage
within yourself to face any challenge.
You have the strength within yourself
to make a difference...

You have the uniqueness within
yourself to be extraordinary.

Be Open
to All of Life's
Possibilities

Let **sunshine** surround you
and sparkling **stars**
lead you to your dreams.
Let **Rainbows** be your guide.
Let your smile lift you up
like a **balloon** in the air
and keep you on your toes.

Open your **life**
to **all** the things
that are coming your way.
Let the **good** times in,
and don't be afraid
to **chase** life's
great **adventures**.
They're guiding you
to your **dreams**.

What the FiRST-EVER BiRd Taught the WORld

When the gROund falls
out fRom below you...

...learn to fly.

If you have never **failed**...
then you probably have not been
"fighting" in the right "weight" class —
with the **best** competition.
♡ If you have never been hurt...
then you have **probably** never gone
after **something** you loved.
If you have never been **frightened**...
then you have probably never put
yourself on the line or **cared** about
something enough to — **win or lose** —
simply give it **everything** you've **got**...
you know: give it your all.
If you have never **fallen**... then
you have not grown or learned how
to get up. ★★☺ If you have never
lost... then you **probably**
have not **taken** enough **chances**...

So if learning and living
involve so **much**
failing and faltering...
how do you **know** if
you're ever doing anything right?

Because **when** you fall –
you fall, but **your heart**...
it dances.

Hold On to Your Dreams

Oh, but for flying elephants and impossible staircases and weeping willows and talking walruses — where would we be? Oh, but for laughing alphabets and silly stories and mad rabbits dancing across the skies — what would get us through the nights? Oh, but for the will to read and dream and dance and paint in between the lines — how could we say that something was not lost?

Hold on to your dreams;
they are as PRECIOUS as laughter —
they are eternal, like STARS.

A Little Advice from Penelope

If you are not sure
which **way** to go...

ask your **heart** –
your heart
will **know.**

When your **mind**
does not know
what to say...

your heart will
find a way.

When you can't **see**
the finish line
or when your **dreams**
seem hard to find...

Know that **you**
know the way:
your **heart** will
lead you **there**
one day.

Each day you can
   start again.
You are free to make
   your way in this world.
You are free to lose.
You are free to win.
You are free to let loose
   in this world
and to laugh as much as
   you want.
You are free to face
each day as if it were
the first day of your life.

What Makes You Different?

You are **unique**, it's true...
There is no one else quite
like **you**. So don't hesitate
to step out from the crowd,
to show your own **style**,
your own **smile**, your **own**
way of doing things...

Individuality is one of the gReatest gifts in life.

You are a girl who changes minds,
takes chances, turns heads, and listens.
You are the first to arrive, the last
to leave, and the first to lend a hand.
You are a girl who remembers,
pauses, makes an effort, and laughs.
You are unique, irreplaceable, and real.

Always be yourself...
for no one else
can compare to
the integrity of
your own
heart.

People turn to you because you give **voice** to dreams, notice little things, and make otherwise impossible imaginings appear **Real**. You are a **Rare bird** who thinks the world is **beautiful** enough to try to figure it out and who has the **courage** to dive into your wild mind and go **swimming** there.

You are someone who still **believes** in cloud watching, people watching, **daydreaming**, tomorrow, favorite colors, silver clouds, **dandelions**, and sorrow. Be **sacred**. Be cool. Be **wild**. Go far.

You are a
girl
who is...

1. sharp
2. talented
3. real
4. brave

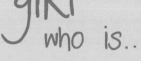

5. remarkable
6. independent
7. incredible
8. daring

You can <u>do</u>
anything!

You **belong** to a long **line**
of **women** who began as
girls **dReaming** –
and gRew up **keeping** on
believing –
and gRew up to be **women**
of intellect, **couRage,**
vision, cReativity…

...women who **make**
a **difference**.

And as far as I can tell...
you are well
on your way
to becoming
one such **woman**.

GRowing Up Is HaRd

Growing Up is
not easy to do...

but each time you
grow...

you learn something
new.

And each **time** you
grow...

you get a little bit
CLOSER...

to your **dReams**
coming true.

GROwing up is
not easy to **do**,
but it's woRth it.

Don't think that it's such a terrible thing to get sad or down or to stop believing in **sunshine** for a while. Don't worry **too much** if you feel empty or lost or you can't make yourself want to **smile**.

Don't think that it's not **okay** to want to **sit** a day out or to be scared or tired or **blue**. **Everybody** gets sad sometimes. And crying and hurting — just like laughing and dreaming — are just **things** that people do.

How to Stay Strong

Take some time every day
to Remember the things
that make you happy...
Whether it's the flowers
outside your door or the wind
Rushing through the trees...
a moment or a smile
or the last time you spent
a really long time laughing.
Hold these things close
in your heart...

They'll keep you strong.

A Few Words from Penelope

I want to tell you that you are **talented** and ambitious. I want to tell you that you are **wise** beyond your years.

I want to say that you are **skilled** and have an instinct for what you do.

I want to say that you are brave, **true,** and **sincere**.

I want to tell you to keep your **spirit** and love for **life** — and that you will go far.

I want to tell you that you're **better** than just **good**...

You're great!

DReam like You Mean It

Many people speak of dreams as **fanciful** things, like **fairies** and charmed rings and lands of enchantment. Others only believe in faraway dreams, such as stars or sea castles with elf-like inhabitants.

There are daydreamers and night dreamers who dream up make-believe places. They use much imagination, and in that way, they are dream gifted. But the serious dreamers are those who catch dreams and bring them to life to show that when they were dreaming, they meant it.

Many have "failed" not from **acting** on their **dreams**, but by silencing their ideas due to a fear of the **unknown** — by not acting at all.

FROM one dreamer
to another...
don't give up.

One day, you will find that all the **daydReams** you planted when you weRe small have **blossomed** into **giant** sunfloweRs. One day, you will turn around and see the **woRld** at your front **dooR**. One day, you will **move** mountains and write your name **acRoss** the sky.

Penelope on
What It Takes
to Be Great

Some people just accept what is handed to them in life — be it very much OR very little — and fashion a WORld out of that.

Other people make their way through the passing days determined to grow up and one day give something back...

Whether **they** know it or not,
these people often open up **doors** for
others, ask questions, and change
lives and minds too... for they **believe** in
bright stars in **everything** they do. They're
tough and kind and amazing and **true**. And
they **never** give up.

That's _you_.

YOUR STAR

There is a **star** in the **sky**...
just for **you**.
That star will make sure
that your **dreams**
come true.

So in case you are **stumbling** —
don't get too blue.
That star in the **sky**...
it **believes** in you.

And **in case** you were
wondering...

I do **too**.

(I **believe** in you
and your star.)

You have the ability to
change the world.
Stand up. Stand tall. Speak up.
Always try your hardest.
Trust yourself.
Try to look at the long-term.
Whatever you are doing,
if you love it,
keep on trying.

Don't worry about yesterday...
just be **here** now.
Don't worry about the future
or what it might bring.
Don't worry about the past –
what did or did not happen.
Be here now
where you are needed...
where anything
can happen.

doctor

sister

artist

friend

princess

goddess

angel

astronaut

daughter

writer

girl

president

woman

athlete

You can be anything!

You aRe an amazing **giRl** with **style** and couRage. You aRe an amazing giRl with big **dReams** and lots of things to do.

How to Reach Your Dreams

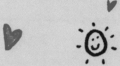

1. Work hard.

2. Study hard.

3. Learn as much as possible.

4. Laugh.

5. Have fun.

6. Make your future your own.

Take These Things with You Wherever You Go

friendship

fun

love   hope

a belief in your dreams

a belief in your goals...

and a **determination**
to get **you wherever**
you need to go.

Winning Your Own Heart

Find a little happiness.
Find a little hope.
Find a little or even a very big
    place where you can go.
Find a little (or big) but very
    excellent dream.
Find some true and some
    Real fun.
If you can do these
    five things...

    ...you've won.

You are an **incredible** girl.

 May your heart
always **dance**.

Penelope on Why
You Gotta Have Hope

You gotta **have hope**
and you gotta **keep trying**
and you gotta keep **believing** that
everything you are striving for
and trying to **do** is worth something.
You gotta have some **heart**
and you gotta **have drive...**
but **mostly** you gotta have **hope...**

...and **hope** comes
from **inside**.

If You Were a...

If you were
a ⭐ star....

you'd be the
🌞 brightest one.

You'd be the
Rare Rainbow
if Rainbows
were 💜 few.

If you were
an answer...

you'd be the ✔
😊 Right one.

You'd be
the perfect
fit, if you were
a shoe.

If you were
a fine 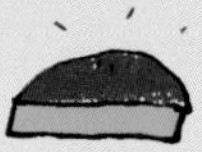
pie...

you'd be the
finest one.

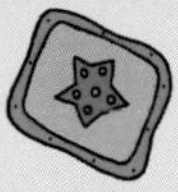

You'd be nice
as the  sunshine
that makes the
sky blue... 

but you're you...
which is better
than all these
things put together.

What You've Got

A **graceful** intellect...

A true and strong character...

A **brave** sense of wit
and humor and
knowingness...

The **guts** to go...

The heart to believe
and to live
and to **dream.**

And **style**, baby —
style.

If someone were to **WRITE**
a book about you,
it would be a
book about...

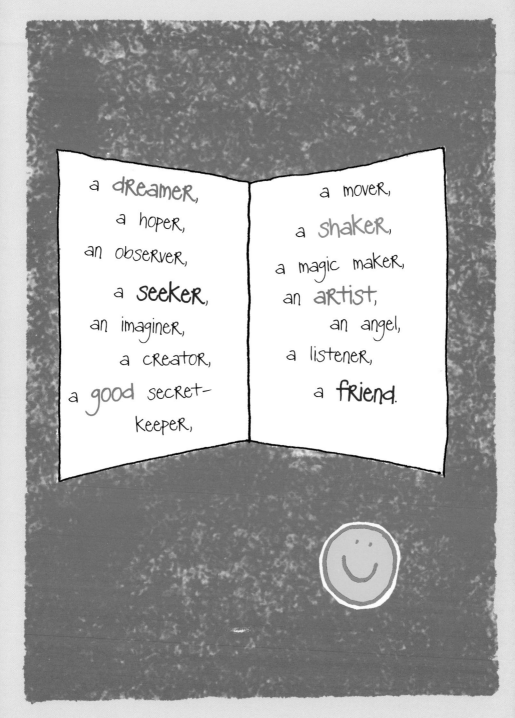

a dreamer,
a hoper,
an observer,
a seeker,
an imaginer,
a creator,
a good secret-
keeper,

a mover,
a shaker,
a magic maker,
an artist,
an angel,
a listener,
a friend.

You are your own
best **adviser**,
your own best judge of
your **heart**...
your own best
dream maker, mapmaker,
and compass.
You are your own
best go-getter and your
own best **cheerleader**
when things are going rough.
You are you...
and that's more than enough!

You go, girl...
you fly.

Believe in your dReams.
Believe in who you are.
Make choices with your brain.
Make decisions with your **heart.**
Define a finish line.
Finish what you start.
Make friends and
make everything you do
worth doing.

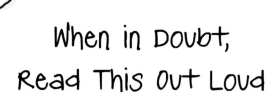

When in Doubt,
Read This Out Loud

I won't be any less than
my **best**.

I won't stress over
small things when
I know that tomorrow
they **can't** hurt me.

And I'll **keep** pressing on
to see **everything**
I know I will see...

Because **I believe** in my life
and I believe in **tomorrow**...
in my heart and in my **dreams**.

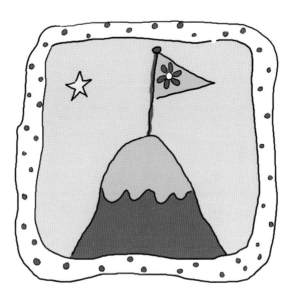

Daisy Power

A daisy is a very
special **flower** that needs
sunlight,
dreams,
and goals
to grow up
strong...
and it's clear
to me that
you've got
daisy
power...

'cuz, girl, your dreams
are growing by the
hour.

This World Is Lucky
to Have a Dreamer like You

You are such an **important** person.
You make a **brighter** day for others,
and even strangers benefit
from the **light** of your smile.
You make a difference
to those **around** you all the time.
You are brave and **wondrous**,
and you **never** give up
when the going gets tough.

You are an **example**
and a shining star and an **angel**.
You are lighthearted
yet **engaged** and passionate
about the things around you.
You are **outgoing**
and caring and strong.
You are a **miracle** in this world,
and it is **lucky** to have you.

A star
for all you do...

A star because
you're bright...

A star to watch over
your days and dreams
each and every night...

A star because
you're unique...

A star because
you're kind...

A star because
you're you:
keep on shining bright!

A Few Last Words
from Penelope

Be the **best** that you can be
at what you do.
Take a step
in the **Right** direction.
Hold on to **good** feelings
and get rid of the bad.
Take a **chance** on a star,
and slide down rainbows.
Forgive yourself
and move forward.
Let in **laughter**.
Say what you mean.
Feel good about who
and where **you** are.
Don't let past mistakes
trip you up.
Seek out happiness
every day.

Believe in everything
you **can** accomplish.
Remember who you are.
Trust in yourself.
Be **open** to adventures.
Ask for help
when you need it.
Look for **miracles**
and angels.
Step on **wishing** stones.
Do everything with **heart.**
Open your mind.
Seek fulfillment
in every way.
Reach for your **dreams,**
and never let them go.

dreams

The more **challenges** that you face...
the more **races** that you **run**...
the more hills that you **climb**
to the **top** and **overcome**...
the **stronger** grows your **heart**,
the **wiser** becomes your **soul**.

Each **time** you **travel**
down a **bumpy** or unknown **road**...
the **swifter** become your **feet**:
with **every** hard-won,
honest **victory** –
and yes, **even** with each **defeat**.

You Can Do Anything

Stay **positive** no matter what
is going on in your **life**.
Life **never** gives us more
than we can handle,
and **you** are more than up to the **task**
of facing **whatever** challenges
may come your way.
You've got a **brilliance** inside you
that outshines any **star**.
Never forget who you are,
what you **stand** for,
or what you've been **through** before.
All these things will strengthen your **spirit**
and **help** you out as you make your way
into new **adventures**
and **stand up** to adversities.

There is **nothing** that
you can't overcome
with **strength** of heart
and a little bit of **courage**.
You are a unique
and **talented** individual
who has everything it takes
to **succeed** in this life.
Just believe in yourself
with **everything** you've got,
and you will find **greatness**
in **every way**, every day.

You are an
amazing girl...

and you can make
your dreams come true!